Our Planet's Most Endangered Wildlife

Kesem Books

"Time is running out for countless species. Their fate is in our hands." - Unknown

www.SavingEndangereSpecies.org

THANK YOU

Thank you for choosing our book! Scan the code below to unlock your FREE thank-you gift as a token of our gratitude.

Your support means the world to us as we passionately strive to raise awareness to saving endangered species. We firmly believe that education and knowledge are the vital first steps.

We hope you enjoy this book, please consider leaving a review on Amazon; your feedback supports us and helps others discover our book.

THIS BOOK
BELONGS TO:

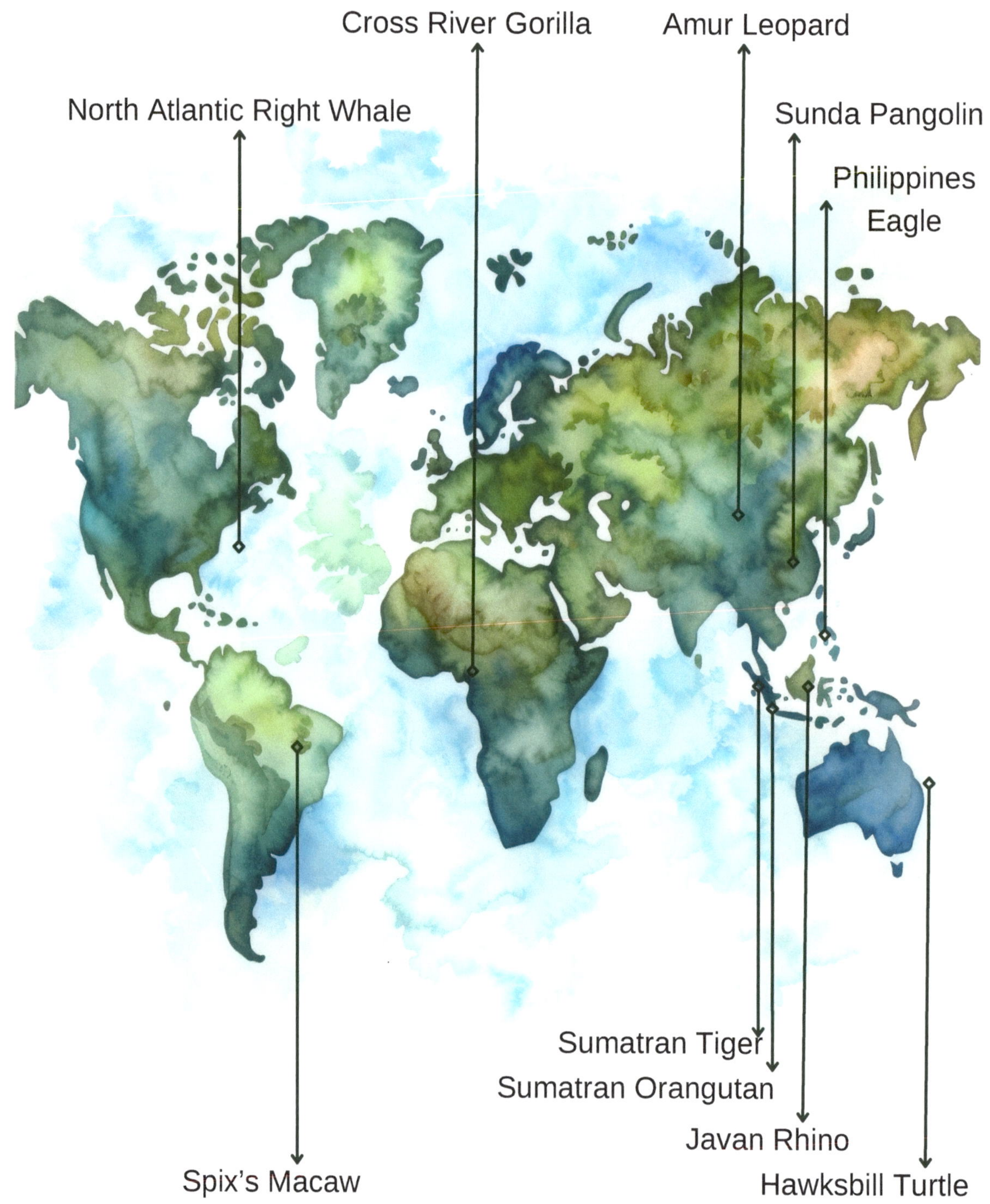

North Atlantic Right Whale
Cross River Gorilla
Amur Leopard
Sunda Pangolin
Philippines Eagle
Sumatran Tiger
Sumatran Orangutan
Javan Rhino
Hawksbill Turtle
Spix's Macaw

TABLE OF CONTENTS

Introduction 7

What Are Endangered Species ? 8

Why Are Species Becoming Endangered? 10

Who Are the Most Endangered Species? 12

Amur Leopard 14

Hawksbill Turtle 16

Cross River Gorilla 18

Spix's Macaw 20

Javan Rhino 22

Sumatran Tiger 24

Sundra Pangolin 26

Phillipine Eagle 28

North Atlantic Right Whale 30

Sumatran Orangutan 32

How Can We Take Action? 34

Learn More and Book Resources 36

DON'T LET THEM

DISAPPEAR

INTRODUCTION

Welcome to the world of Endangered Species! In the pages of this book, we invite you on a journey to discover some of Earth's most precious and endangered inhabitants that are in need of our help.

You will learn about these unique and vulnerable beings and the challenges they face. But this book is more than just a collection of facts and stories; it's a bridge to a world where you can make a real difference. By understanding the importance of preserving these species, you'll be better equipped to take action and join the global effort to protect them.

As you read on, you'll discover that knowledge is your greatest tool in the fight for conservation.

Visit our website for additional resources, information and to connect with a community of like-minded individuals committed to safeguarding the natural wonders of our planet. Together, we can raise awareness, foster appreciation and ensure a brighter future for these incredible creatures.

What Are Endangered Species ?

Endangered species are animals or plants that are at risk of disappearing forever.

Being endangered means that a species is in danger of extinction throughout all or a significant portion of its range.

Once a species goes extinct, it is gone forever, and there is no going back.

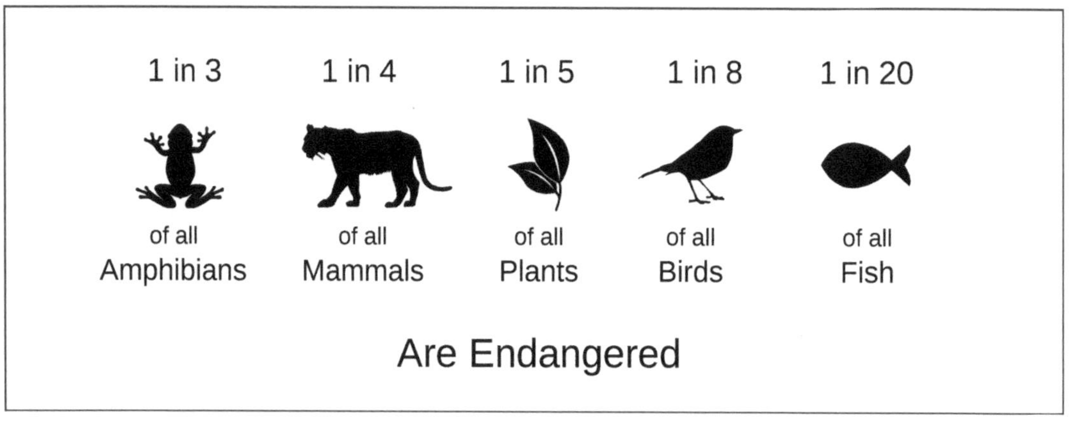

More than 42,100 species are threatened with extinction which are almost a third of all the assessed species worldwide.

Endangered species share several characteristics that make them vulnerable to extinction:

First, they often have a small population, which makes them susceptible to environmental changes & genetic problems.

Second, they have a limited geographic range, which means they only live in a small area, making them vulnerable to habitat loss and other threats in their living area.

Third, they often have specialized habitat requirements, which means they need a specific type of environment to survive, making them even more vulnerable to habitat loss and degradation.

Fourth, they often have low reproductive rates, which means they have fewer offspring and take longer to recover from population declines.

Finally, they are often threatened by human activities such as habitat destruction, pollution, and over-harvesting.

Why Are Species Becoming Endangered?

There are many reasons why species become endangered, here are a few of the most common reasons:

Loss of Habitat

This happens when the place where a species lives is destroyed or changed so much that it can no longer survive there. This can happen naturally, but it is often caused by humans who cut down forests, build cities, or pollute the environment. For example, when forests are cut down, the animals that live there lose their homes and food sources, making it difficult for them to survive. Similarly, when wetlands are drained, the plants and animals that live there are forced to find new homes, which can be difficult or impossible.

Loss of genetic variation happens when a species population becomes too small, there are fewer individuals to mate with, which can lead to inbreeding. Inbreeding can cause genetic problems, such as birth defects and reduced fertility. In addition, the reduced genetic diversity can make a population more vulnerable to diseases and environmental changes.

Over-harvesting when humans hunt or fish too much, it can cause a species to become endangered. This is often the case with animals that are hunted for their fur, meat, or other products. For example, many species of whales were hunted to near extinction for their oil and meat.

Pollution can harm or kill animals and plants, making it harder for them to survive. Pollution can come from many sources, including factories, cars, and agricultural runoff. For example, when oil spills occur, the oil can harm or kill marine animals and plants. Similarly, when pesticides are used on crops, they can harm or kill insects and other animals that are important to the ecosystem.

Who Are the Most Endangered Species on our Planet?

The most endangered species are determined by various organizations, including the International Union for Conservation of Nature (IUCN), which maintains the **Red List of Threatened Species**.

The Red List defines the severity and specific causes of a species' threat of extinction and has seven levels of conservation: least concern, near threatened, vulnerable, endangered, critically endangered, extinct in the wild, and extinct.

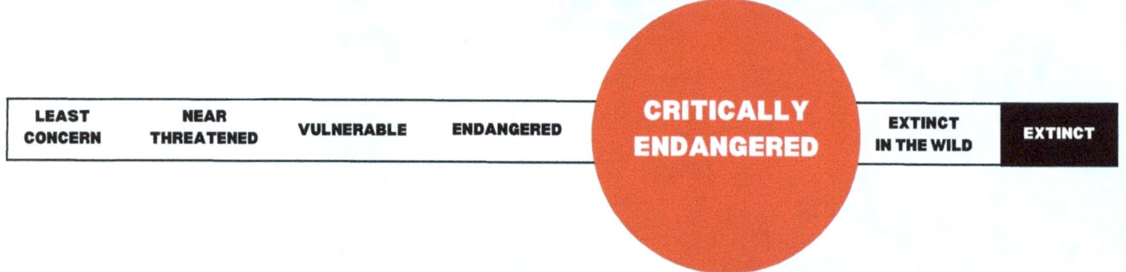

The classification of a species as endangered has to do with its range and habitat, as well as its actual population. For this reason, a species can be of least concern in one area and endangered in another.

The most endangered species on our planet are those that are classified as critically endangered, which means they face an extremely high risk of extinction in the wild, in all areas.

To determine the absolute "most" endangered species, you would need to consider factors such as the size of the remaining population, the rate of decline, the extent of their habitat loss, and the severity of threats they face. These factors can change over time, and new assessments are regularly made by conservation organizations and experts to determine the current status of various species.

In this book we chose to focus on ten examples of critically endangered species. Unfortunately, there are many more endangered species facing critical threats. Conservation efforts are needed to protect all threatened species, it is up to us to take action to protect them.

AMUR LEOPARD

The Amur Leopard is one of the rarest big cat species, with possibly fewer than 100 individuals remaining in the wild.

The Amur Leopard's original habitat stretched from China to Russia. However, habitat loss is a major threat facing this leopard. People are turning forests into farm-land and towns, cutting down trees for farming and roads. As a result, the leopard is losing its home and the places it needs to survive. This shrinking and fragmentation of its habitat are putting the leopard in serious danger.

Because of this habitat loss, the leopard's range has greatly decreased. Now, it mostly lives in a small area within the cold forests of Russia. The Amur Leopard is able to survive this cold with its thick fur coat that helps keep it warm. This coat can have shades of yellow and orange, and it's covered in spots that form a unique pattern which help it hide and camouflage with its forest surroundings.

The Amur Leopard faces another main threat from poaching, as some individuals desire its stunning fur and body parts. This demand drives people to hunt leopards, selling their products on the black market, where illegal trade occur.

LEAST CONCERN
NEAR THREATENED
VULNERABLE
ENDANGERED
CRITICALLY ENDANGERED
EXTINCT IN THE WILD
EXTINCT

HAWKSBILL TURTLE

Scientists consider the Hawksbill Turtle as highly vulnerable to extinction.

The Hawksbill Turtle is one of the world's most critically endangered sea turtle species, with merely around 8,000 nesting females. Its name is derived from the narrow, pointed beak it possesses, and its shell showcases a remarkable pattern of overlapping scales that give its edges a serrated appearance.

One of the most concerning challenges facing Hawksbill Turtles is their targeted hunting for their prized shells, often referred to as "tortoise shell." In the past millions of these turtles were hunted to supply the tortoiseshell markets of Europe, the United States, and Asia. Even today, despite efforts to curb both domestic and international trade in tortoiseshell, the trade still remains a main threat for these turtles.

Hawksbill Turtles confront additional threats including the loss of their nesting and feeding habitats due to development of coastal areas, excessive collection of their eggs and mortality linked to fishing activities. Sea turtles need to reach the surface to breathe, therefore entanglement in gill nets and accidental capture on fishing hooks further challenges these remarkable creatures.

LEAST CONCERN
NEAR THREATENED
VULNERABLE
ENDANGERED
CRITICALLY ENDANGERED
EXTINCT IN THE WILD
EXTINCT

CROSS RIVER GORILLA

Africa's most endangered great ape, with only between 200 and 300 individuals left in the wild.

The Cross River Gorilla, a Western Gorilla subspecies, inhabits the mountainous border region between Cameroon and Nigeria, near the headwaters of the Cross River, from which it derives its name.

These gorillas are shy and tend to avoid human contact, making direct scientific study challenging. Researchers have relied on indirect indicators like nest counts and estimated range sizes, concluding that only about 200 to 300 of these gorillas remain in the wild.

The primary threat to the species is habitat loss due to deforestation and habitat degradation. Many Cross River Gorilla groups live in unprotected forests, facing the risk of habitat loss through logging as local communities clear land for agriculture and cattle grazing.

Hunting also poses a significant threat to the Cross River Gorilla, as it is targeted for its meat and body parts. Moreover, the subspecies faces the danger of inbreeding and a loss of genetic diversity due to its small population size and limited genetic exchange between subpopulations. Additionally, these gorillas are vulnerable to diseases such as Ebola, which can have devastating impacts on their already small and isolated population.

LEAST CONCERN
NEAR THREATENED
VULNERABLE
ENDANGERED
CRITICALLY ENDANGERED
EXTINCT IN THE WILD
EXTINCT

SPIX'S MACAW

Spix's Macaw is critically endangered and no longer lives in the wild, making it the world's rarest macaw.

The Spix's Macaw is native to Brazil, originally found in the dry, scrubby forests of the Caatinga region. However, this region is under significant threat, with over half of its original vegetation already lost due to human activities such as agriculture, cattle ranching, and logging.
The result of this habitat destruction, also known as habitat loss, is that natural habitats can no longer support their native species. The Spix's Macaw's natural habitat is directly impacted, presenting a significant challenge for its survival. The reduction in available space for the birds to forage, nest, and breed has significantly diminished their chances for survival.
In addition to habitat loss, the Spix's Macaw faces threats from illegal trade, as it is a highly sought-after bird in the pet trade. The bird's rarity and distinctiveness make it a prime target for illegal trade, with a high demand for it in the pet market leading to the capture of birds for sale.
Conservation initiatives are actively working to save the Spix's Macaw from extinction. These efforts include a captive breeding program and the protection of their habitat. The long-term goal for conservationists is to reintroduce Spix's Macaws back into the wild in their natural habitat

LEAST CONCERN
NEAR THREATENED
VULNERABLE
ENDANGERED
CRITICALLY ENDANGERED
EXTINCT IN THE WILD
EXTINCT

JAVAN RHINO

The Javan rhinoceros is a critically endangered species with only around 70 individuals remaining in the world.

The Javan Rhino is the most threatened of the five rhino species, and it is found in only one protected area in the world: Ujung Kulon National Park in Java, Indonesia.

Their habitat once extended across the lush forests of Indonesia. However, human activities such as agriculture, logging, and development have led to the destruction and fragmentation of the Javan Rhino's habitat. This loss of habitat severely impacts the rhinos, limiting their ability to move, find food, and mate.

Today, the biggest threat to the Javan rhino is its very small population size, which leads to inbreeding and the loss of genetic diversity. This could make it extremely challenging for this species to survive diseases or natural catastrophes.

Poaching is another major threat to the Javan rhino, as it has been hunted for its horn, which is highly valued in traditional medicine and as a status symbol. This destructive demand drives individuals to hunt rhinos and sell their body parts on the black market, where illegal trade thrives. This detrimental trade further endangers the survival of this critically endangered species.

LEAST
CONCERN
NEAR
THREATENED
VULNERABLE
ENDANGERED
CRITICALLY
ENDANGERED
EXTINCT
IN THE WILD
EXTINCT

SUMATRAN TIGER

The Sumatran Tiger is classified as Critically Endangered, with less than 400 individuals estimated to be surviving in the wild.

The Sumatran Tiger is a critically endangered subspecies of tigers that is native to the Indonesian island of Sumatra. They have darker orange fur and stripes that are closer together, allowing them to blend into their tropical rainforest habitat. The Sumatran Tiger lives in low and highland areas, mountainous jungles, and peat swamp forests.

The greatest threats to the Sumatran Tiger are habitat loss, human-tiger conflict, and poaching.

The habitat of the Sumatran Tiger has been drastically reduced by clearing the forests for agriculture, particularly oil palm plantations, and forest conversion for human settlements.

As the human population expands, humans are living closer to tigers than ever before, leading to conflicts. Tigers are often caught in snares set by villagers to catch wild pigs or deer, leading to severe injuries and death. In addition, people injuring and killing tigers in retaliation for the loss of livestock poses another threat to this species.

Poaching is driven by the illegal trade of tiger body parts, which are used in traditional Chinese medicine and sold as trophy items. These are worth billions of dollars annually and are the third most profitable trade on the black market.

LEAST
CONCERN
NEAR
THREATENED
VULNERABLE
ENDANGERED
CRITICALLY
ENDANGERED
EXTINCT
IN THE WILD
EXTINCT

SUNDA PANGOLIN

This species is critically endangered and has declined by 80% between the years 1998 to 2019.

The Sunda Pangolin, also known as the Malayan Pangolin, is a critically endangered scaly mammal species found in Southeast Asia. The Sunda Pangolin possess a distinctive appearance, characterized by their armor-like, scaly skin and elongated snouts. They are equipped with large, curved claws for digging and tree climbing, while their prehensile tails aid in branch-clinging. Sunda Pangolins are solitary, timid, and predominantly nocturnal, seeking refuge in tree hollows or burrows during the day. They exhibit excellent climbing abilities and are even adept swimmers.

The most significant threat to the Sunda Pangolin across its habitat is hunting and poaching. Pangolins are captured using snares or trained detection dogs, primarily for the international trade of live animals, skins, and scales to China and Vietnam, where their scales are utilized in traditional medicines, and their meat is considered a delicacy in restaurants.

Another major threat for the Sunda Pangolin is habitat loss. As their natural habitats are destroyed, Sunda Pangolins are compelled to adapt to new environments or face the risk of extinction. This poses a significant challenge for the species as they are highly specialized and rely on specific habitats for their survival.

LEAST
CONCERN
NEAR
THREATENED
VULNERABLE
ENDANGERED
CRITICALLY
ENDANGERED
EXTINCT
IN THE WILD
EXTINCT

PHILIPPINE EAGLE

There are only 400 breeding pairs of Philippine Eagles left in the wild.

The Philippine Eagle is one of the largest and most powerful eagles globally, with a wingspan of up to 7 feet (2 meters). This magnificent species is indigenous to the Philippines, specifically found on the islands of Luzon, Samar, Leyte, and Mindanao. They inhabit the country's tropical rainforests, where they construct their nests on top of large trees and require extensive territories for both hunting and breeding. The Philippine Eagle is a monogamous species, with pairs typically remaining together for life. Notably, they exhibit a slow reproductive rate, with females laying just one egg every two years.

The Philippine Eagle faces numerous threats primarily due to habitat loss resulting from deforestation, illegal logging, and mining activities. These actions significantly diminish the availability of suitable territories for these regal birds.

Additionally, the Philippine Eagle confronts the threat of hunting and trapping for the illegal wildlife trade. Their substantial size and imposing appearance make them a target for trophy hunters.

As a top predator within the Philippines' food chain, the Philippine Eagle is vulnerable to poisoning, the use of DDT-based pesticides effected the eagles too, leading to instances of cancer, and malformed chicks.

LEAST CONCERN
NEAR THREATENED
VULNERABLE
ENDANGERED
CRITICALLY ENDANGERED
EXTINCT IN THE WILD
EXTINCT

NORTH ATLANTIC RIGHT WHALE

One of the world's most endangered whale species, with an estimated population of only about 350 individuals.

This baleen whale feeds by filtering small organisms such as krill and copepods from the water. These majestic creatures are migratory, traveling from their feeding grounds in the North Atlantic to their breeding grounds in the southeastern United States.

North Atlantic right whales are renowned for their slow swimming pace and their frequent presence near the water's surface, making them highly vulnerable to the perils of ship strikes and entanglement in fishing gear.

The most significant threat these whales face is human-caused mortality and injury, primarily due to entanglements and vessel strikes. In fact, entanglement in fishing gear is responsible for roughly 58% of the species' fatalities. Climate change presents another serious threat to these whales, with the potential to alter their migratory patterns and affect the availability of their food sources. Warming oceans can disrupt the essential food sources for the whales' survival.

LEAST CONCERN
NEAR THREATENED
VULNERABLE
ENDANGERED
CRITICALLY ENDANGERED
EXTINCT IN THE WILD
EXTINCT

SUMATRAN ORANGUTAN

The Sumatran Orangutan is one of the rarest great ape species, with possibly fewer than 7,000 individuals remaining in the wild.

The Sumatran orangutan inhabits the island of Sumatra in Indonesia. One of the main threats to the Sumatran orangutan is the loss of its natural habitat due to conversion of rainforests for agricultural purposes. The destruction and degradation of the tropical rainforests pose a significant risk to orangutans, pushing them towards the brink of extinction. Habitat fragmentation is another pressing concern for orangutans. Even the simple act of cutting a road through a forest can divide an orangutan population in half, even if the forest on either side remains relatively intact. Orangutans are highly sensitive to environmental changes, making fragmentation particularly detrimental to their survival.

Poaching is another threat to the orangutans, despite the illegality of capturing or keeping young orangutans as pets, they are still highly sought after. This illegal trade puts their populations at even greater risk, further challenging their survival.

LEAST CONCERN
NEAR THREATENED
VULNERABLE
ENDANGERED
CRITICALLY ENDANGERED
EXTINCT IN THE WILD
EXTINCT

33

TAKING ACTION

There are many ways that you can help protect endangered species and their habitats. Here are some things you can do to make a difference:

Learn about endangered species in your area:
The first step to protecting endangered species is learning about how interesting and important they are. Learn about the threats and challenges they face. You can teach your friends and family about the wonderful wildlife, birds, fish, and plants that live near you.

Create a backyard wildlife habitat: You can establish a pollinator garden or a bird feeder in your backyard to attract and support local wildlife. This can provide a safe place for animals to find food, shelter, and raise their young.

Reduce, Reuse, Recycle: You can reduce your impact on the environment by reducing your use of single-use plastics, recycling, and composting. This can help reduce pollution and protect habitats.

Don't litter or destroy sensitive habitats: You can help protect endangered species by not littering or otherwise destroying sensitive habitats, which may be home to native or visiting species that are endangered or threatened. You can also organize or participate in a "clean up" campaign of an important habitat in your area.

Advocate for stronger environmental policies: You can write letters to your local newspaper or elected officials to advocate for stronger environmental policies. This can help protect endangered species and their habitats from threats like habitat destruction, pollution, and over-harvesting.

By taking these actions, you can help protect endangered species and their habitats. It is important to remember that every little bit helps.

Even small actions can make a big difference.

LEARN MORE & BOOK RESOURCES

There are countless books and websites where you can discover a wealth of knowledge about Endangered Species. We highly recommend beginning your journey with the following resources, which have also been instrumental in shaping this book:

American Bird Conservancy
Britannica Encyclopedia
International Union for Conservation of Nature
National Geographic
National Oceanic and Atmospheric Association
One Kind Planet
World Land Trust
World Wildlife Foundation

To learn more about endangered species visit our website:
www.SavingEndangeredSpecies.org